PUFFIN BOOKS

LAUGHTER IS AN EGG

To say laughter is an egg may not be the most obvious image to draw; but in John Agard's brilliant, witty and evocative collection of poems which explore the nature of laughter, it turns out to be a surprisingly appropriate one. Jokes crack like eggs, riddles are hatched, and egg monsters come down from the sky in this unique book that provides non-stop, thought-provoking entertainment.

John Agard was born and lived in Guyana until 1977 when he moved to Britain. He worked for the Commonwealth Institute for several years giving talks, readings and work-shops, but is now a freelance writer and performer of poetry for both adults and children. He lives in Sussex with the poet, Grace Nichols.

D0182972

John Agard

Laughter is an Egg

Illustrated by Alan Rowe

PUFFIN BOOKS

For Grace
With Loveter

PUFFIN BOOKS

Published by the Penguin Group
Penguin Books Ltd, 27 Wrights Lane, London w8 5tz, England
Viking Penguin, a division of Penguin Books USA Inc.
375 Hudson Street, New York, New York 10014, USA
Penguin Books Australia Ltd, Ringwood, Victoria, Australia
Penguin Books Canada Ltd, 2801 John Street, Markham, Ontario, Canada l3r 1b4
Penguin Books (NZ) Ltd, 182–190 Wairau Road, Auckland 10, New Zealand

Penguin Books Ltd, Registered Offices: Harmondsworth, Middlesex, England

First published by Viking 1990
Published in Puffin Books 1991
10 9 8 7 6 5 4 3 2 1

Text copyright © John Agard, 1990
Illustrations copyright © Alan Rowe, 1990
All rights reserved

The moral right of the author has been asserted

Printed in England by Clays Ltd, St Ives plc
Filmset in Century Old Style (Linotron 202)

Contents

Once Upon a Time

Once upon a time there lived
a small joke
in the middle of nowhere.

This small joke
was dying to share
itself with someone

but nobody came to hear
this small joke.

So this small joke told
itself to the birds

and the birds told this small joke to the trees
and the trees told this small joke to the rivers
and the rivers told this small joke to the mountains
and the mountains told this small joke to the stars

till the whole world
started to swell with laughter

and nobody believed
it all began
with a small joke

that lived in the middle of nowhere.

Everybody kept saying

it was me
it was me.

Where Does Laughter Begin?

Does it start in your head
and spread to your toe?

Does it start in your cheeks
and grow downwards so
till your knees feel weak?

Does it start with a tickle
in your tummy so
till you want to jump right out

of all your skin?
Or does laughter simply begin

with your mouth?

Laughter's Chant

HA-HA-HA-E-E-E-O
HA-HA-HA-E-E-E-O
HA-HA-HA-E-E-E-O
IN SUNRISE
IN MOONGLOW
I COME I GO
NOW YOU HEAR ME
NOW YOU DON'T.

HA-HA-HA-E-E-E-O
HA-HA-HA-E-E-E-O
HA-HA-HA-E-E-E-O
FROM WIND I COME
TO WIND I GO
IN YOUR EYES
I MAKE RAIN
IN YOUR EYES
I MAKE RAIN.

HA-HA-HA-E-E-E-O
HA-HA-HA-E-E-E-O
HA-HA-HA-E-E-E-O
THUNDER I MAKE ROAR
AT THE DOOR
OF YOUR MOUTH
THUNDER I MAKE ROAR
AT THE DOOR
OF YOUR MOUTH.

HA-HA-HA-E-E-E-O
HA-HA-HA-E-E-E-O
HA-HA-HA-E-E-E-O
ALL RIGHT SAD FACE
I WILL COME AGAIN
TO WRINKLE YOUR NOSE.

Laughter is an Egg

Laughter is an egg
that does a one-leg hop

Laughter is an egg
that can outspin a top

Laughter is an egg
with a crick-crack face

that can hide in the heart
of the human race.

How Laughter Made Clock Smile

To make Clock smile
even a little smile.
That's what Laughter wanted to do.

So Laughter stared at Clock
Clock didn't.

Laughter clapped hands
Clock didn't.

Laughter made a funny face
Clock didn't.

Laughter asked Clock
have you any idea of the time?

Clock chuckled.

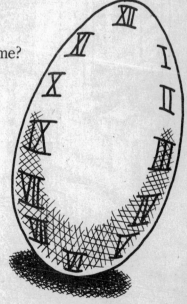

Bogeyman Headmaster

Our headmaster is a bogeyman
Our headmaster is a bogeyman
and he'll catch you if he can.

He creeps through the window
when the school is closed at night
just to give the caretaker a fright.

Our headmaster is a bogeyman
Our headmaster is a bogeyman
and he'll catch you if he can.

When he walks
his feet never touch the ground.
When he talks
his mouth never makes a sound.
That's why assembly is so much fun.

You should see him float through the air
when we say our morning prayer
and at assembly the teachers get trembly
when the piano starts to play on its own.
It's our bogeyman headmaster having a bogeyman joke.

Only the lollipop lady doesn't feel scared
cause when he tried his bogeyman trick
she said, 'Buzz off or I'll hit you with my stick.'

Life can be lonely
for our bogeyman headmaster
but from his office you can always hear
this strange sound of laughter.

I Know You Wouldn't
Think I'm Serious

'Teacher, Teacher,
There's an egg in the computer!'
                              the child cried.

'Teacher, Teacher,
There's an egg on the piano,'
                              the child cried.

'Teacher, Teacher,
Look! An egg is on the blackboard,'
                              the child cried.

The teacher sighed
and told the child to stand
outside the headmaster's office.

Just then the headmaster burst into the class.
He was laughing and wringing his hands
and saying to the teacher

'I know you wouldn't think I'm serious,
but do you know there's an egg standing outside my
     door?'

Laughter's Morning Advice

So you crack eggs
So you crack jokes

So why not start your day
with scrambled jokes on toast?

Laughter's Night-Time Advice

After you brush your teeth
and you're ready for bed

LAUGH BEFORE YOU LEAP

into sleep

and if you can't sleep
don't count sheep

try counting grass instead.

Laughter Looks
at Banana Skins

Banana skins are vicious!
They make you slip and fall flat.
No, I take my word back,
I wouldn't call them that,
Banana skins are not vicious

        Just

             mischievous . . .

Laughter and the Magician

The magician tried
to pull Laughter
out of a hat.
Laughter said enough of that
I'm no rabbit.

The magician tried
to put Laughter
into a box
and run a sword through.
Laughter said try something new.

The magician tried
to get Laughter
to lie down flat
I'm going to saw you in two.
Laughter said is that all you could do?

The magician replied
I will make you disappear
into thin air.
Nothing will remain of Laughter
Not one trace of you.

Laughter rolled Laughter hopped
You'll make me disappear
when an egg becomes square.

The magician cried and cried
and covered his face
with his top hat.

The crowd laughed
to see an egg
make a magician crack.

23

Don't Say a Word

Don't say a word to Turkey
Don't say a word to Duck
Don't say a word to Hen
But Laughter swop de eggs
from inside dey pen.

Now Turkey sitting on eggs belonging to Hen
and Duck sitting on eggs belonging to Turkey.

Meanwhile, Hen on Duck eggs going CLUCK
    CLUCK CLUCK.

O what a confusion when eggs done hatch
and Mother Hen find she baby a-go QUACK
    QUACK QUACK
and Mother Turkey find she baby a-go CHEEP
    CHEEP CHEEP
and Mother Duck find she baby a-go GOBBLE
    GOBBLE GOBBLE.

Only one egg remained unhatched.
And all it did was WOBBLE WOBBLE WOBBLE.

Laughter at the Supermarket

Round and round in supermarket circles
ain't much fun,
but weekend shopping must be done.

Every Friday, same old story
staring at things like cabbage and broccoli,
when all you want is crisp and lolly.

Hear Dad: That's a nice piece of braising steak.
Hear Mum: This shopping always gives me a
        headache.
Hear Dad: Don't know why you never make a list.
Hear Mum: Must pick up some cherries for the cake.

What about crisp and lolly?
And bet they'd say no
if you ask to have a go
at pushing the trolley.
But what can you do when you're only two?

Only sit trapped in little trolley basket,
round and round in supermarket,
and wait for your turn to get to the queue.

When will they reach crisp and lolly
underneath cabbage and broccoli
and that big big big box of soap powder?
O how you wish they'd hurry.

Suddenly Mum and Dad are in a flurry.
Hear Dad: Look what you've done, silly.
Hear Mum: You've broken one of the eggs, Billy.

Round and round in supermarket circles
ain't much fun,
but you like it when an egg is smiling.

Laughter's Boast

Not a box in the world
Not a tin in the world
can lock me in
said Laughter with a grin

Not a rope can tie me
Not a chain can bind me
just try to lock me in
said Laughter with a grin

Show me the peg to pin me
Show me the bolt to bar me
Show me the cage to confine me
just try to lock me in

Fat or thin
even skeletons enjoy
a grin

Egg-and-Spoon Race

One school sports day,
in the egg-and-spoon race,
        the egg ran away
        from the spoon.

The egg brought first place
but the judges said: 'Let's disqualify
the egg.
It should have waited on the spoon.'

The egg said: 'Why not disqualify
the spoon
for not catching up with me?
I'll never understand the mystery

        of the human race.'

Laughter and the Elements

Fire and Water
Wind and Earth

These four elements
I will forge into myself
said Laughter

Till the wind of breath
will fill your lungs

Till the water of tears
will flood your eyes

Till the fire of blood
will flush your face

Till the whole of your body
will roll on earth

your legs weak with giggles.

Alien Humour

A visiting alien from out of space
could not understand the jokes
that Earthlings make.

'When they throw a pie in the face,
is this a greeting from the human race?

And why do most Earthling comics stand up,'
asked the alien with a frown,
'when it's more comfortable to tell jokes lying down?

Another thing I've noticed,' said the alien amazed.
'Why do you throw eggs at your politicians
when they say things that make you angry?
Where I come from eggs are so wonderfully precious
we throw them only on festive days
and only at those who make us smile and keep us
        happy.'

'Well, I'm tickled pink,' said one Earthling.
'Know what I mean?'

'Maybe,' replied the alien. 'And I'm tickled green.'

Laughter Will Return

The old man and old woman cried
when their dog died.
They had that dog from a pup.
They watched that dog grow up.

That dog was once their friend.
Now that dog is dead.

From the house of the dead
Laughter has gone.
To the house of the dead
Laughter will return.

Aunty Grouchy

Aunty Grouchy was so grouchy
she could not stand
to see children happy.
Children, she said, need a ruling hand.

If they sat down too relaxed
she'd tell them sit up.
Don't be slouchy.
Can't you sit like your Aunty Grouchy?

If she sent them on an errand
she'd tell them make it snappy.
I am waiting
and I haven't got all day.

If they bounced a ball
against the wall
she'd say I can't be hearing what I'm hearing.
Put that ball away.

If she heard them laughing
she'd remind them of the saying:
Laugh before breakfast, cry before nightfall.
I think you'd be better off praying.

The children thought of putting
a spider in her bedding,
but then they remembered Aunty Grouchy made
such wonderful egg-and-custard pudding.

No Answer

Once the seals had skins
shiny wet as a new anorak.

Now their skins have a rusty look
of an old car part.
The star has fallen out of their eye.

The seals have no answer
to the question
of poisonous waste.

O Laughter
walk on water
that the seals may smile again.

Spell to Bring a Smile

Come down Rainbow
Rainbow come down

I have a space for you
in my small face

If my face is too small for you
take a space in my chest

If my chest is too small for you
take a space in my belly

If my belly is too small for you
then take every part of me

Come down Rainbow
Rainbow come down

You can eat me from head to toe

A-So It Go

So mouthy-mouthy
so mouthy-mouthy
you got so much
MOUTHABILITY!
A-so it go
A-so it go
when yuh mouth can't stop flow

So wanty-wanty
so wanty-wanty
you got so much
WANTABILITY!
A-so it go
A-so it go
when you wanty dis and wanty dat

So laughy-laughy
so laughy-laughy
you got so much
LAUGHABILITY!
Take care one day you laughy-laughy
till you burst
yuh belly-belly

Prayer to Laughter

O Laughter
giver of relaxed mouths

you who rule our belly with tickles
you who come when not called
you who can embarrass us at times

send us stitches in our sides
shake us till the water reaches our eyes
buckle our knees till we cannot stand

we whose faces are grim and shattered
we whose hearts are no longer hearty
O Laughter we beg you

crack us up
crack us up

Laughter Playing Cards

Crick-crack
break my back

Shuffle de cards
in de pack

I'll make your
king sticky
and your
queen too

I'll even glue
your ace to
your jack

For I'm de
joker in de
pack

How Laughter Helped
Stop the Argument

FIRST VOICE: *Look at the clouds*
                so fluffy
                so sheepy
                That's because God
                got woolly hair.

SECOND VOICE: *Look at the rain*
                falling strands
                falling everywhere
                That's because God
                got straight hair.

THIRD VOICE: *Look at de sun*
                look at de moon
                That's why
                God got a yellow eye.

FOURTH VOICE: *Look at the sea*
                look at the sky
                That's a clue
                God's skin must be blue.

FIFTH VOICE: *What about the night*
                that wraps us dark
                and makes us sleep tight?
                God's skin must be black.

SIXTH VOICE: *What about the snow?*
                Oh no, God's skin must be
                    white.

THIRD VOICE: *No, God's skin must be green*
                look at de trees
                See what I mean.

FIRST VOICE: *Well, then since you are all so*
                    clever
                just answer me
                Is God a father or a mother?

SECOND VOICE: *A father.*

FIFTH VOICE: *A mother.*

SIXTH VOICE: *No, a father.*

THIRD VOICE: *How about a grandmother?*

AND WHILE THESE SIX VOICES
WERE ARGUING AND ARGUING
JUST THEN A SEVENTH VOICE STEPPED
    IN

Listen my friends
and listen well
crick me your ears
and I'll crack you a spell

God might be a story
with no beginning
and no end

God might be laughter
for all you know
God might be a HA-HA-HA-HAaaaaaaaaaaaa
      a HO-HO-HO-HOoooooooooooo
      a HE-HE-HE-HEeeeeeeeeeeee
      a SHE-SHE-SHE-SHEeeeeeeeeeeee

               a million million
                  laughing pebbles
                  inside of
                     you and me.

That's what God might be.

Where Laughter Hid
God's Drum

Of course it was Laughter
who took God's drum
and hid it under
the elephant's bum

And from the skies
came the mighty question
WHO THIEF MY DRUM
          MY THUNDER-DRUM?

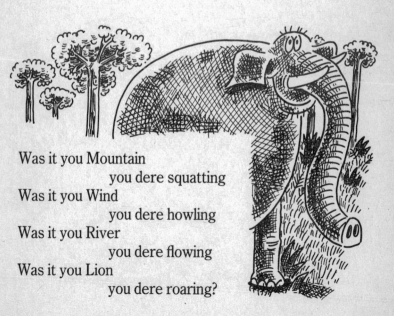

Was it you Mountain
          you dere squatting
Was it you Wind
          you dere howling
Was it you River
          you dere flowing
Was it you Lion
          you dere roaring?

43

Yet again from the skies
came the mighty question
WHO THIEF MY DRUM
          MY THUNDER-DRUM?

Who was it I wonder?

No answer

But God didn't think of looking
                    over yonder

under the elephant's bum

Laughter's Favourite Animal

I agree
rabbit is sweet
and chimpanzee
is very clever,
and you'll never beat
elephant for memory.

If you see
fierce tiger
you'd wish
you could run like ostrich,
or better yet had the feet
of cheetah.

Sure, parrot could chatter,
snake could change skin,
and for a pet
some would pick hamster.
For creepy-crawly feet
you might place a bet
on spider to win.

But alligator
has that special something.
Teeth that seem to laugh
Teeth that seem to grin.

Laughter at Dinner

Laughter crept in
through a hole
in the doughnut

and sat one-legged
on an empty plate.

The rich owners
of the house
were embarrassed
but began to shake

because Laughter
had not been invited
but Laughter had chosen
their most expensive plate.

How they began to shake and shake
wishing the butler
had not seen them in this state!

Which Came First?

Which came first
the chicken or the egg?
Some say the chicken
Some say the egg.

If you didn't have an egg
to hatch from the very start
how could you have had a chicken?
But then again, without a chicken
you wouldn't have had an egg.

The argument goes on and on.

But one bright little egg
with a mysterious nod
says the very first egg
was laid by God

and mislaid by the Devil.

So whether the very first chicken
was hatched in heaven or hell

no one can tell.

Meet Me at Sundown

Meet me at sunrise
meet me at sundown
meet me any time
any place you choose

Send out de funniest clown
in de town
send out de best jester
in de west
I'll put him or her to the test
in this bloodless duel of a contest

We'll laugh with we belly
we'll laugh with we chest
we'll laugh till we knees turn jelly
we'll laugh each other out of breath
in this the world's
first laughing duel to the death

But win or lose, it won't matter,
no blood will splatter,
and the first to die of laughter
will be buried
in the land of HAPPY-EVER-AFTER.

First Morning

I was there on that first morning of creation
when heaven and earth occupied one space
and no one had heard of the human race.

I was there on that first morning of creation
when a river rushed from the belly of an egg
and a mountain rose from a golden yolk.

I was there on that first morning of creation
when the waters parted like magic cloth
and the birds shook feathers at the first joke.

Hatch Me a Riddle

In a little white room
all round and smooth
sits a yellow moon.

In a little white room
once open, for ever open,
sits a yellow moon.

In a little white room,
with neither window nor door,
sits a yellow moon.

Who will break the walls
of the little white room
to steal the yellow moon?

A wise one or a fool?

I Didn't Mean To

I didn't mean to laugh so loud
I made the windows rattle
and your jam jar split in two.
I didn't mean to laugh so loud
I made your best plates scatter
and your picture twisted on the wall.
I didn't mean to laugh so loud
your budgie flapped against the cage
and the television stopped.
I didn't mean to laugh so loud
the bulbs in your house just went POP.

Mummy always said that if I don't change my laugh
people will never invite me back to their house.

But when I grow up I'll change my name to

THUNDER.

Ballad of Count Laughula

Dead on the stroke of the midday bell
Count Laughula rises
from his merry shell.

Midday sky resounds with a crack
and Count Laughula plans
another side-splitting attack.

Draped in pudding-yellow cloak
that wobbles in the wind
Count Laughula sharpens a deadly joke.

This is a Count that does not haunt by night
but prefers to stalk a victim
in broad daylight.

When a judge throws off his wig and laughs HA-HA-
    HA
you can bet he's been bitten
by none other than Count Laughula.

When your teacher gets stitches in her side
and leans on the desk
you know she has been Count Laughula's bride.

When a Prime Minister demands a lollipop
in the middle of a speech
Count Laughula is surely getting on top.

He is the vampire that makes you laugh
and all over the city
he'd sign his mysterious autograph.

And when sun goes down, hook or crook,
Count Laughula returns to his shell
safely tucked in with a comic book.

Welcome Home

An old lady found an egg
in her garden bed.

Suddenly a voice cried
let me out, let me out.

Curious, she broke the egg
to see what was inside.

Out hopped a tiny man
– a garden gnome.

'O welcome home,'
the old lady smiled.

'Among my roses
You can lay your head.'

The Soldiers Came

The soldiers came
and dropped their bombs.
The soldiers didn't take long
to bring the forest down.

With the forest gone
the birds are gone.
With the birds gone
who will sing their song?

But the soldiers forgot
to take the forest
out of the people's hearts.
The soldiers forgot
to take the birds
out of the people's dreams.
And in the people's dreams
the birds still sing their song.

Now the children
are planting seedlings
to help the forest grow again.
They eat a simple meal of soft rice
wrapped in banana leaf.
And the land welcomes their smiling
like a shower of rain.

Superstitious Darling

A lonely old man boiled an egg
scooped out the yellow
filled the white with salt instead
ate the egg before going to bed
placed the shell under his pillow
and hoped to dream of the one
he would some day wed.

'If I don't marry soon,' he said,
'I'd rather soon be dead.'

That night the old man died in his sleep
but from his lips there came a song:

'I'll meet you, my darling, it won't be long.
I'll be your darling, your dancing egg,
I'll be your darling, your spick-and-span egg,
I'll be your darling, your cuddling egg,
a-rolling over the water
a-rolling over the water.'

Some people say they still hear the old man's song.
Who are we to say if they are right or wrong?

The Eggshell

The eggshell had the look of an ancient grin.
No one knew the how or where of it.
It could not be traced to bird or wind or sand.

Better leave it alone. Better not walk over it.

But the little girl skipped over the eggshell.
The little girl hopscotched over the eggshell.
The little girl back-flipped over the eggshell.

Now her parents wonder why she cannot stop grinning.
Even when she's asleep, her face seems to crack
as if amused by some ancient thing.

Laughter Rap in Plastic Town

One day as I was passing through plastic town
I happened to pass a school playground
yet I couldn't hear one laughing sound.

Can you imagine a school playground
and not a single laughing sound?
But that's how it was in plastic town.

For though they were playing as children play,
plastic children do so in a most unusual way.
Not one was laughing, not one I say.

Every move they made was made of plastic
it was sad to see children so robotic.
They could do with a touch of my laughing magic.

So I reached for my hip-hop cap
got into my egg-leg tap
broke into my laughing rap.

Children, children of plastic town
it makes me sad to see you frown.
Cracking up with laughter is the thing to do,
cracking up with laughter makes you feel brand-new.
So give me a crick, give me a crack,
just throw yourself into the laughing act.

I promise my magic will bring you right back.

How Laughter Helped Steal Fire

Long long ago when Alligator was fire-keeper
Alligator keep fire all to heself
hide fire in the deep of he mouth
hide fire like a red red secret.

So the animals come together
to form a plan to thief de fire.
If only we could make Alligator laugh,
in this way he must open that big mouth,
and one of us could snatch the fire out.
Elephant try telling elephant jokes.
Anteater try telling anteater jokes.
But Alligator mouth stay stiff as a post.
Wise Owl didn't even bother to try.
Nobody could understand wise Owl jokes anyhow.
But wise Owl come up with a suggestion
that got the birds perking up their heads.
Yes, yes, yes, that should make Alligator laugh:
Let's ask Monkey to pee upon our eggs.
Of course, Monkey willingly obliged
and the sight of Monkey acting so naughty
made Alligator laugh so hearty
that he open he mouth wide wide wide

AND OUT FLEW FIRE IN A BLAZE OF
    LAUGHTER.

Inspired by a South American Indian myth

The Clown's Last Joke

Whatever became of the clown's red nose?

They found a farewell note
in a bundle of tricks

They found a shaggy eyebrow
under a floppy hat

They found a painted cheek
inside a grinning shoe

They found a rubber ball
between baggy trousers

But they never found the clown's red nose

They pulled out drawers
They turned over sheets

But whatever became of the clown's red nose
only God in heaven knows

A Clown's Conclusion

We are born. We grow up.
We laugh. We cry.
Then when the egg
inside us stops beating,
it's quite simple. We die.

A Clown's Thought

Beneath my clown's disguise
there are things in my eyes
resembling diamonds.
But they don't sparkle.
They burn.

Laughter's Haiku

The clown hid two eggs
between his legs.
O naughty naughty man.

Why?

The man without a head
He laughed his head off.

The woman without a head
She laughed her head off too.

But what can they do?
Life isn't fair.

O why can't they laugh
their heads back on again?

The Clown's Wife

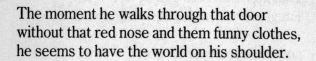

About my husband, the clown,
what could I say?

On stage, he's a different person.
Up there he's a king on a throne,
but at home you should hear him moan.

The moment he walks through that door
without that red nose and them funny clothes,
he seems to have the world on his shoulder.

I do me best to cheer him up, poor soul.
I juggle with eggs, I turn cartwheels,
I tell jokes, I do me latest card trick,
I even have a borrow of his red nose.

But he doesn't say exactly how he feels,
doesn't say what's bothering him inside.
Just sits there saying almost to himself:

'O life, ah life,
what would I do without this clown of a wife?'

Laughter Can

Laughter can be hairy
Laughter can be smooth

Laughter can be polite
Laughter can be rude

Laughter can catch you by day
Laughter can catch you by night

and don't you ever forget
Laughter can make you wet yourself

Flying Egg

An enormous egg was coming
in a swirl of wind
towards the earth!
How strange, thought Earthlings.
Earthlings ran. Earthlings panicked.
Earthlings hid in fear.
Earthlings did not dare
face this egg monster,
which landed on a hill-top
with a spectacular plop.
Earthlings, of course, did not guess
that it was only God trying out
an egg-shaped balloon
filled with heavenly gas.
Earthlings who had invented rockets
were now scared at the sight
of a flying egg!
The sky shook with big laughter
as the egg disappeared into golden light
that caused Earthlings no harm.

And from that day on
Earthlings called the hill –

EGG-SATELLITE HILL.

Index of First Lines

Some other Puffins

LAUGH YOUR HEAD OFF!
Martyn Forrester

How to outwit your French teacher, how to survive a school trip to France – just two of the subjects in this hilarious and original book.

CROSSWORD CRACKERS
Colin Gumbrell

A carefully thought out, original and inventive collection of crosswords with clues covering a wide range of general knowledge.

PUZZLER'S A TO Z
Colin Gumbrell

Puzzle your way from A to Z with these inventive and entertaining anagrams, word searches, shape and number puzzles, crosswords and quizzes of all kinds.

THE GREAT PUFFIN JOKE DIRECTORY
Brough Girling

Over 1,000 jokes presented alphabetically with Fat Puffin to guide you through. An original, hilarious book – you'll never be short of a laugh again!

CHUCKLE, CHUCKLE, THE CHILDREN'S JOKE BOOK
Ann Leadercramer and Rosalind Morris

An original and entertaining collection of jokes, puzzles and riddles from St Anthony's School, Hampstead, in aid of the Wishing Well Appeal.

UP WITH SKOOL!

A book of jokes from children themselves, divided into ten sections including school dinners, homework and exams, and introduced by Mr Majeika.

THE HA HA BONK BOOK

Janet and Allan Ahlberg

This joke book is full of good jokes to tell dads, mums, baby brothers, teachers, and just about anybody else you can think of!

THE D-I-Y GENIUS KIT

Gyles Brandreth

An hilarious guide on how to gain the entire world knowledge – all in one box! With amazing facts at your fingertips you can stun your friends – and we guarantee that absolutely no mental equipment is necessary!

THE CHRISTMAS STOCKING JOKE BOOK

Shoo Rayner

A joke book that every child will enjoy, packed with lots of festive jokes and cartoons.

THE SECOND PUFFIN CROSSWORD PUZZLE BOOK

Alan Cash

Another challenging crossword puzzle collection, including specialist puzzles for experts in science, literature and loads of other subjects. There are plenty of cryptic and general clues, too – enough to keep all crossword addicts happy.

CAN YOU GET WARTS FROM TOUCHING TOADS?

Doctor Pete Rowan

TV-AM's Doctor Pete answers questions that children ask him on every subject from warts to hiccups, to the speed at which a sneeze travels.

WORD PUZZLES

David Smith and Veronica Millington

An entertaining collection of puzzles covering a wide variety of areas of interest.